COUNTRY BROCANTE
Style

COUNTRY
BROCANTE
Style

LUCY HAYWOOD

PHOTOGRAPHY BY
BEN EDWARDS

RYLAND PETERS & SMALL
LONDON • NEW YORK

Senior designer Toni Kay
Senior commissioning editor
 Annabel Morgan
Location research Jess Walton
Head of production
 Patricia Harrington
Art director Leslie Harrington
Editorial director Julia Charles
Publisher Cindy Richards

First published in 2019 by
Ryland Peters & Small
20–21 Jockey's Fields,
London WC1R 4BW
and
341 East 116th Street
New York, NY 10029

www.rylandpeters.com

Text copyright © Lucy Haywood
2019
Design and photographs copyright
© Ryland Peters & Small 2019

10 9 8 7 6 5 4 3 2

ISBN 978-1-78879-084-0

A CIP record for this book
is available from the British
Library.

Library of Congress CIP
data has been applied for.

Printed and bound in China

CONTENTS

INTRODUCTION

My passion for vintage treasures started at an early age. My parents spent all their free time at antiques fairs and I grew up in a home filled with old furniture. My grandfather had the most beautiful house in West Sussex, and as little girls my sister and I would spend hours looking at his most treasured pieces, all kept safely locked away in his precious glass cabinet. My father took me on buying trips at the crack of dawn, searching for antique fishing tackle and treasures to take home to mum. This sparked a passion for treasure hunting that has stayed with me ever since!

My friend Fred and I spent much time in our young adult life jumping into his vintage car and bombing down country lanes to get to vintage fairs and car boot/yard sales. My first flat was adorned with antique finds and vintage clothing and I realized that I was, of course, going to be drawn to a creative career. After a wonderful start designing at British Airways, I found myself in interiors heaven at OKA, followed by various commercial roles within creative businesses. My father has always been full of entrepreneurial spirit, which I seem to have inherited, and growing up listening to the talk of business around the kitchen table eventually led me to start my own venture.

When my daughters were tiny, I wanted to create a business that would work alongside my role as a mum and decided to put my collections to work. I began by hiring out my vast collection of vintage china for weddings and other events. This led to me opening a little shop in Sussex and, as the business grew, I moved to a large, draughty barn, inviting other collectors that I met to sell alongside me. I hosted sales in village halls and gardens, and The Country Brocante was born. Rather than buying and selling myself, I created an event that united carefully chosen sellers with people in search of interesting finds. The Country Brocante has grown and evolved from its humble beginnings. We now host seasonal fairs at stately homes and estates in Sussex and the Cotswolds and have visitors who come from far and wide to enjoy our events.

Our exhibitors specialize in various different eras and styles – some offer classic French *brocanterie*, others have a traditional English style, and some a blend of both. The faded elegance of France and the English cottage charm of vintage china and chintz come together to create a uniquely beautiful look that is, for me, the essence of the Country Brocante style and which I have tried to capture in this book. I hope you enjoy this glimpse into the world of Country Brocante sellers and buyers and will be able to visit us to experience the fairs for yourself!

COUNTRY BROCANTE
Style

THE COLOUR PALETTE

Soft pastels and faded hues are at the heart of the Country Brocante look. Opt for a chalky, subdued palette to harmoniously combine pretty English and French details.

Colour is key when looking for antique and vintage pieces. Whether on a piece of furniture or scrap of fabric, it will often be the colour that first catches a buyer's eye. Vintage textiles, whether French or English, floral or plain, tend to be found after spending years in storage, either folded in trunks or hanging at a window. Softened by the years, their colours are now the perfect muted hue with just a hint of the original shade. Knowing where to find these pieces is also key – being the early bird at fairs and sales means you have the best chance of discovering exciting treasures.

PALE PINKS

Graceful, elegant and feminine, for me pink is the most romantic of colours and effortlessly exudes vintage charm. Even the smallest of details, such as a posy of pink flowers, will bring warmth to an interior. If you aren't keen on large expanses of pink, introduce textiles with a pink print –a ditsy floral Sanderson design or Cabbages & Roses Hatley are subtle ways to add the colour to your interiors. If pastel pink feels too sugary, try a rich raspberry shade instead, which looks fabulous against pearly grey or duck-egg blue walls and natural sisal flooring.

ROSE-TINTED

We discovered covetable pink pieces in many of the homes we visited, such as Amanda Daughtry's kitchen bench, which she bought at Rachel Ashwell's Los Angeles store (this page, bottom left), Susannah Adorian's floral bedroom curtains (top left), and ribbons and trims at Jenny Nicole's home, including these pale pink silk tassels (bottom right). Finding furniture that still has its original pink paint intact can only be described as the icing on the cake (opposite and right, centre left). And, of course, rose-tinted details, such as garden flowers in jam jars or a pile of vintage books, bring country charm to any room (centre right and top right).

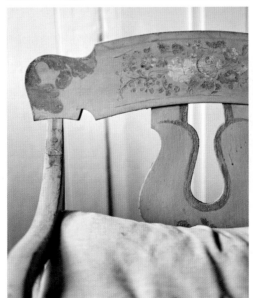

WASHED WHITES

*There is a myth that white is
cold, hard and clinical. In Country
Brocante homes, this is far from
the truth. The secret is to search out
muted, chalky whites that provide
a perfect backdrop for the timeworn
patina of antique and vintage finds.
White-painted furniture only grows
more beautiful with age, and when
it is teamed with old linen sheets,
white sofas and all-white china,
the effect is easy, relaxed and
lived-in. If you have a collection
of mismatching modern pine
furniture, invest in a pot of one
of Farrow & Ball's just-slightly-
off-white shades and give pieces
a lick of paint for instant shabby
appeal. Steph Eley's house
(see pages 92–105) is the perfect
example of an all-white home
with a warm and cosy vibe.*

WHITE OUT

White is very easy to live with but
lots of texture is necessary in a pale
interior to add depth and interest.
At brocantes and antique fairs, look
out for different objects in varying
shapes, finishes and shades – glossy
French ceramics, furniture with flaking
original paintwork and piles of freshly
laundered white bed and table linen
(this page). Who can resist the appeal
of a newly made bed covered with
layers of crisp white linen (opposite)?

SEASIDE BLUES

Blue always brings to mind the sea and the sky and as such can be instantly calming. For a Country Brocante home, seek out subtle shades from silvery pale blue to faded indigo. Blue and white is, of course, found on many a piece of old English or French china, from Willow Pattern to vintage enamelware, as well as in the form of old painted furniture and the sea and the sky in paintings and prints. I found so much of this calm, contemplative colour in the houses featured in this book, with tiny fragments of blue popping up even in all-white interiors.

BLUE MOOD

Sophie Bateman's duck-egg blue shepherd's hut is a dreamy retreat (opposite), while the bluest of skies are to be found in a painting perched at the foot of Susannah Adorian's staircase in Sussex (this page, bottom right). Soft blues are the perfect foil to so many other shades, from warm whites (bottom left) to rusty reds (top right and centre right) and the green of garden foliage (top left). While photographing this book, we unearthed beautiful blue hand-dyed linen and lace in linen presses and cupboards (centre left).

SOFT GREENS

What colour could be more reminiscent of the rolling English countryside than green? It brings to mind the exterior of an old garden shed, lichen and moss growing over a weathered stone garden ornament, or a simple green bucket holding roses just picked from the garden. But green is for indoors as well as out. There are so many shades that work in a country-style home, from faded sage to olive to seafoam. Just keep your shades subtle and sludgy and you can't go far wrong. At the Country Brocantes, a keen eye will seek out the softest, most subtle green pieces, choosing battered enamel buckets and garden chairs to take home and treasure.

GOING GREEN

Green is sympathetic to so many other shades, from warm white to bare wood to the shell pink of freshly picked garden roses (this page). In a French market, Jenny and Simon Nicole of Rosehip in the Country found a wonderful old writing desk that now resides in their bedroom in Suffolk (opposite). It is the most perfect shade of verdigris, the soft and chalky original paint sitting beautifully against the natural bleached wooden beams.

TIMEWORN TEXTURES

What is it we love about the antiques and vintage pieces we collect? For most of us, it is the faded colours and rich patinas that make them so special.

The houses included in this book, whether old Suffolk cottages, Georgian farmhouses or modern properties, all have in common the inclusion of timeworn objects. There are salvaged shutters and doors, shelving fashioned from old scaffolding boards and pieces of painted furniture still clinging on to their original finish, flaking and peeling though it may be. Despite their age and their state of repair, these items manage to look current, exciting and utterly beautiful in their current surroundings.

No two pieces have the same patina and it is impossible to replicate the dimmed colours and the weathered surfaces found on treasured brocante finds. Some people – those who love the shiny and the new – will never understand the attraction of tattered and timeworn pieces, but for those of us who appreciate these items, they possess a charm that cannot be defined.

Antique hunting is all about the journey and the discovery. A piece of furniture with its original paint, a faded scrap of floral fabric or a bundle of old letters is something to treasure and covet. We pick up an old book and wonder who has read it before, stroke the pages and marvel at its age. On a larger scale, tearing down a wall and uncovering original lime plaster beneath or ripping up a dusty carpet to find ancient boards can feel like opening the best present ever on Christmas Day.

ANCIENT TREASURES

Have the confidence to respect your home and its history without needing to 'fix' or 'improve' things. Instead, revel in the rich textures of old fabrics, materials and objects and let them tell their own story (this page and overleaf). The door to Jenny and Simon Nicole's guest bedroom is a perfect example of holding on to original features that have stood the test of time – it still retains traces of an old floral wallpaper and a variety of paint colours (opposite).

VINTAGE TREASURES

*With age comes beauty – vintage treasures and timeworn pieces will
bring a sense of romance, nostalgia and character to any home.*

FINISHING TOUCHES

From galvanized metal dolly tubs to
old linen napkins, foxed mirrors and
stoneware jars, vintage finds bring
soul to an interior and there is no
better place to search for them
than at brocantes or antiques fairs
(this page and overleaf). A slightly
rusty old French garden chair adds
nostalgic charm to a bedroom and
proves the perfect bedside companion
– pretty, lightweight and just the right
size to hold a pile of books and, if
necessary, an alarm clock (opposite).

What is wonderful about vintage
treasures and objects from the past
is that you will rarely find two the
same – you and your neighbour may
have similar tastes, but accessorizing
with vintage pieces means your home
will be truly individual and unique.

I love to give vintage finds a new lease
of life, but I am equally likely to pick
up something purely for its nostalgic
appeal. I have always been drawn to
old teacups and saucers, particularly
lustreware, and have been known to buy
cups without handles, jugs with cracks
and chips and – my favourites – plates
riveted together with antique metal
staples, fixed by an unknown hand,
totally useless but utterly beautiful.

The Country Brocante fairs are
the perfect hunting grounds for these
period pieces. There's something for
everyone, whether your tastes run to
old enamelware, vintage kitchenalia or
original haberdashery/notions – reels of
faded ribbons and sheets of buttons. As
mentioned before, some of us simply
prefer pieces that speak of a previous
life, while other people are inveterate
collectors of one particular item –
French stoneware, vintage quilts or
old-fashioned French cutlery/flatware.

Vintage treasures are perfectly suited
to an older home, but such pieces look
equally good against the clean white
walls of a newly-built property, adding
romance, character and charm.

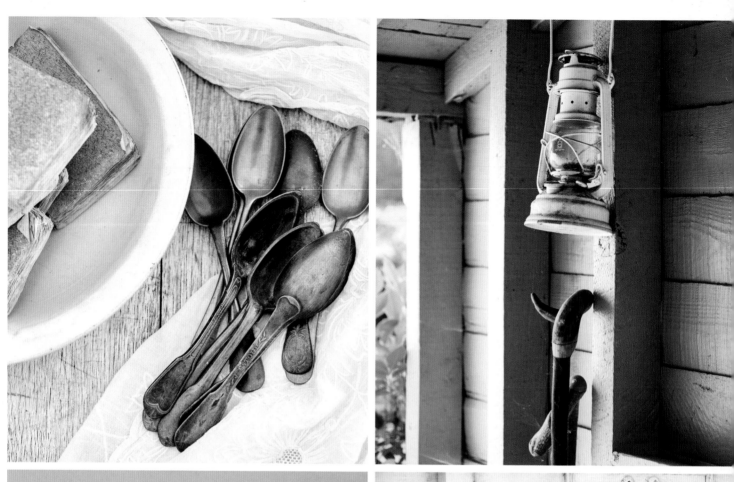

ART

Seeking out vintage and antique paintings and prints at brocantes and fairs can be an affordable way of starting a collection of original artwork.

Who knows what draws us to a work of art and why? Perhaps you may choose a piece because you are attracted to its subject matter – a seascape that reminds you of your childhood – or its faded and muted colours, its naïve charm or because the canvas is so distressed it has become a piece of art in itself.

A collection of vintage oil paintings of flowers, picked up here and there over the years, can be grouped together to make a statement that is greater than the sum of its parts. Or perhaps one large painting depicting soft green rolling hills and chalky blue summer skies will grab your eye. Countryside scenes are evocative of quieter times and I find they have the power to calm

and soothe. When we visited Caroline Zoob's cottage, I was particularly inspired by her collection of seascapes, all in carefully chosen neutral tones.

Of course, art comes in many different forms. Kate Nicole from Oyster Bridge & Co creates delicate floral paintings that she embellishes with handstitching. These hang throughout the farmhouse belonging to her parents, Jenny and Simon, and look perfect against the exposed rustic timbers of the old property. Caroline Zoob's exquisite embroideries adorn the walls of many of the houses featured in this book and are modern heirlooms that will be passed down the generations – the antiques of tomorrow.

ARTFUL ARRANGEMENTS
Unframed paintings have a directness and simplicity that work well in a rustic home. They can be propped up informally on chests and shelves and act as components in decorative vignettes, such as the ones shown above left, opposite and overleaf. Add dried flowers and other natural adornments for a more rustic feel (above centre and right). Many people collect artworks in one particular style or subject matter. Caroline Zoob has amassed a collection of seascapes and displays them above an old drawer unit (overleaf). She has a wonderful eye and these works share a common colour palette as well as subject matter.

ARCHITECTURAL ANTIQUES

We always have stalls devoted to architectural antiques at the Country Brocante fairs, offering up such finds as old doors and shutters, agricultural tools, garden antiques and other gardenalia.

The patina of age is often even more evident on architectural antiques, which have spent most of their lives out of doors. For me, this is all part of their charm. As always, the best pieces are those that are untouched and unrestored with no repainting or rubdowns – exciting finds covered in lichen and verdigris, looking as if they have just been plucked from a rambling chateau garden surrounded by climbing roses. Even the smallest square of garden can be home to such finds. We may not all have space for an antique French garden table, but there's always a corner for a galvanized metal watering can complete with bumps and scratches or a stack of terracotta plant pots.

Using larger architectural antiques such as reclaimed doors is an easy way to add character to an outside space. At Caroline Zoob's new home, an oak door at the top of the garden, which gives the impression that it leads into a secret garden beyond, was found at Ardingly Antique Fair – on spotting it, Caroline immediately knew exactly where she wanted to place it.

Old doors and shutters are perfect for Country Brocante interiors, especially if you live in a house or apartment that lacks interesting architectural features. Michelle Essam used old doors to create a headboard (page 145) while a pair of old French shutters have pride of place in Steph Eley's sitting room (page 92).

GARDEN GLORIES

A beautiful old bench sits in the front garden at Jenny and Simon Nicole's Suffolk house (opposite). It may not be the most comfortable of seats now, but it looks perfect in its surroundings, as though it has always been there, ready for someone to sit and admire the garden. An antique garden roller with beautiful ironwork is a perfect example of a piece that can bring vintage charm to a garden (above left). Smaller pieces, including rustic gardenalia and utilitarian tools such as this stepladder (above centre and right), are among the items worth seeking out to introduce Country Brocante style to your home and garden.

DECORATIVE TOUCHES

You don't need to live in a grand mansion or have a huge budget to feature beautiful decorative details in your home – in fact, many of my favourite pieces have cost pennies.

EASY ON THE EYE

Decorative finishing touches need do no more than enchant or entice the eye. In Steph Eley's kitchen, an old white shelf is home to practical items such as enamel jars, old zinc buckets and a dustpan and brush, but it also holds great visual appeal thanks to the monochrome palette, typographic elements and a dainty vintage clock (opposite). Anything can be used as a decorative detail, from old walking sticks with a lustrous patina to a curious metal light fitting to a dried flower wreath (above, left to right).

Looking for decorative finishing touches must surely be the most enjoyable part of decorating – choosing items based solely on their visual appeal and the whimsy and charm they will bring to our home or to an existing collection. I know many buyers who are obsessed with textiles, but it isn't because they are looking for lengths of curtain fabric or new sheets. Instead, they are on the hunt for the rare and unusual – a quilt in a fabric they have never seen before, or a linen sheet with a perfect mend of miniscule stitches and a dainty patch. For them, these are precious gems that will be taken home and gloated over, put on display or set aside to await a future project.

It is wonderful to observe how our homeowners' collections and displays reflect their vision and creativity. Amanda and Belle Daughtry are drawn to romantic items, and colour is key – soft pinks, blues and chalky whites. These look perfect in their whitewashed cottage, among Rachel Ashwell Shabby Chic fabrics and vintage furniture (see pages 48–57). I was particularly taken with Barbara Cunnell's mini-museum – precious finds that she couldn't part with, the fruit of a lifetime's collecting, all displayed on a handpainted shelf unit (see page 128). All the items in the display are reflected in the colour palette used throughout the house, showing her cohesive decorative vision.

ALL IN THE DETAIL

One of my favourite decorative pieces is a bucket given to me by my sister, who discovered it at Sunbury Antiques Market. She knew I would love its ancient patina and delight in filling it with roses from my garden. Here it is, standing beside one of my many piles of textiles and an antique hat I found at the Country Brocante summer fair (opposite). In the homes we visited for this book, there were a multitude of decorative flourishes to be seen, from dainty teacups (top left) to a pair of tiny metal angel wings (above left). Caroline Zoob's linen-lined basket was home to vintage haberdashery/notions, including threads, lace and buttons in

faded sepia hues (above, top centre), sitting beside a piece of her embroidery (above centre). Textiles are my weakness, and I coveted many of the antique quilts we saw draped over sofas, armchairs and beds – Emma Gurmin's home was filled with quilts, each one exquisite (top right). Fresh flowers are the perfect finishing touch, like these peonies in Sophie Bateman's home. Their pastel tones work well with a Country Brocante palette (above right). Thoughtful decorative details such as these and the pretty vignettes shown overleaf make a house a home and give an insight into the inhabitant's personality.

PUTTING IT ALL TOGETHER

*Starting to collect antique furniture, vintage treasures and decorative details
is only the first step. Now you have to put it all together in your own home.*

So you've visited your first brocante, chosen your colour scheme, decided to embrace your raw, unfinished pine floorboards and are wondering where to put your new French tureen or embroidered footstool. Or perhaps you've been visiting car boots/yard sales, vintage fairs and antiques markets for years and have amassed a huge amount of old-fashioned tools or haberdashery/notions – how best should you style and display them all?

First of all, remember that opposites attract. Placing contrasting textures close to each other plays up their

individual features – think of a plush velvet cushion beside raw plaster or unfinished wood. Equally, the rough texture of a stone carving will highlight the sleek finish of polished marble. In a new home such as Barbara Cunnell and John Taylor's (see pages 128–137), the orderly modern architecture and clean white walls provide an understated backdrop for her collection of decorative antiques, while in Susannah Adorian's home, the elegant, refined Georgian shades on the walls set off the vast rustic beams perfectly (see pages 118–127).

When it comes to smaller items, bear in mind that a collection of objects or items arranged en masse will always have more impact than a display of just one or two pieces, which can look a little timid and underwhelming. Amass handfuls of old wooden spoons in a creamware jug, layer three or four old quilts across a bed or line up a whole row of enamelware canisters or storage jars along your kitchen countertop.

Tabletops, shelves and other surfaces offer an opportunity to create your own decorative vignettes – experiment with objects of different scale, shapes and textures until you stumble upon something that pleases your eye. Arranging and rearranging your treasures can become addictive and it's a soothing, meditative pastime. Look out for furniture such as sideboards, shelving units and glazed cabinets that can house growing collections or particular favourites, like Emma Gurmin's wonderful Swedish armoire, which houses her French tableware (see page 150).

I hope that the homes featured in this book will provide ample styling inspiration and ideas for how to put things together, whether you find yourself drawn to the simple, pared-down style of Amanda Daughtry (see pages 46–57), the opulent elegance of Lou Mora (pages 66–77) or the cosy, layered, rustic look that characterizes the home of Michelle Essam (see pages 138–145).

STYLING SUGGESTIONS
Play with contrast: plump cushions and layered quilts soften the strong verticals of the wooden beams in an attic bedroom in Jenny Nicole's home (page 42), while a dry branch brings organic shape and colour to Barbara Cunnell's pared-down, tranquil spare bedroom (page 43). Piles of fabric tucked into small shelves and a shelf holding mismatched china create a cosy, cluttered vibe in Michelle Essam's home (left), but all the pieces are linked by their pastel palette. Lou Mora's drawing room has a more austere, elegant vibe but every surface offers an opportunity for an exhibition of favourite pieces (above left and opposite).

COUNTRY
BROCANTE
Interiors

OPPOSITE The dining room is decorated in chalky white tones that create a clean and simple backdrop for the carefully chosen furniture. The stand-out piece here is a stunning wooden bench that Amanda fell in love with at Rachel Ashwell's Shabby Chic Los Angeles store and brought back home with her. It is painted pink with floral details and accessorized with a wonderfully plump feather cushion in duck-egg blue velvet.

RIGHT The kitchen is minimal and pared back, in keeping with Amanda's design discipline. Some colour and detail are introduced via pieces of simple hand-thrown pottery and garden flowers. Through the open door you can just glimpse the traditional pantry, stocked with supplies stored in Mason jars.

PRETTY RUSTIC

I love the way Instagram allows us to peep into people's homes and be inspired by their creativity. I met mother and daughter Amanda and Belle Daughtry many years ago through the Country Brocante and we bonded over a love of all things vintage. However, it was not until the arrival of Instagram that I really got to know their style and followed their move from an Edwardian townhouse to a picture-perfect cottage in rural Suffolk.

'As our children started to leave home, the townhouse was too big and we fancied a change,' Amanda explains. 'It took about three years to find our cottage. We hadn't been searching in Suffolk, but Belle saw it online and we decided to have a look. As soon as we saw the cottage, we fell in love with its charm and the surrounding countryside.'

The Daughtry family – Amanda, husband Richard, Belle and their little dog Peppa – set about immersing themselves in country life. Their cottage was built in the seventeenth century with a few later additions and is Grade II listed. A pretty white gate invites you into a quintessentially English garden, brimming with lavender, roses and peonies. In May, the walls of the cottage are almost eclipsed by wisteria flowers. There is a very old pond, which is listed in the deeds, and a small orchard

OPPOSITE The sitting room is filled with an L-shaped white denim sofa from Rachel Ashwell, surrounded by pretty pastel furniture with its original paint and patinas. The paintings on the wall are by Laurence Amélie and strike a feminine note that's emphasized by the floral displays around the room.

ABOVE AND RIGHT One of the most charming features of the cottage is that each bedroom is accessed via its own steep little staircase. The warm, natural tones and textures of these staircases and the original brick floors, the exposed bricks in the inglenook and the sandblasted beams all come together to create a relaxed country feel that works perfectly with Amanda's rustic antiques and the faded colours of the rugs.

dotted with wild flowers. The property is located down a lane, surrounded by fields and farmland yet is only 15 minutes from the sea, making it the perfect rural idyll.

With their love of flowers and calm, serene interiors, the house is a perfect fit for Amanda and Belle. 'What we loved so much about the cottage was that the original features had been embraced. The beams were left exposed, the original brick floors were intact and all the walls were already white,' Amanda recounts. The look they have created is clean and simple, almost minimal, with much-loved vintage china and fabrics tucked away in painted cupboards. Yet the overall feel is comfortable and cosy. Generous white sofas fill the sitting room, a space for family and friends to be comfortable in, but do not detract from the calming feel of the room. Delicately coloured fabrics adorn the windows and freshly-cut flowers appear throughout, bringing little bursts of colour to pale countertops and quiet corners.

The proportions of the cottage are tiny, so all the furniture was carefully sourced and measured to ensure it would fit through the doorways and windows and work within the rooms. The low ceilings meant that the family were unable to hang the beautiful chandeliers from their old home, but Amanda and Belle

RIGHT Below the internal window, which looks through to the kitchen, a white-painted unit found at an antiques fair provides valuable storage space. Amanda has resisted the temptation to overload it, instead piling up stacks of books and magazines and topping it with small vases of fresh flowers and a lamp with a delicate lace shade.

OPPOSITE Creativity abounds in Belle's photographic studio. Dried flowers picked in the summer months hang from the beams and give the space a charming feel. Pinboards are covered with pretty postcards and photographs providing inspiration.

RIGHT The studio is decorated in Belle's signature pastel shades. A sofa bed has been fashioned from a simple wooden slatted base. A Cabbages & Roses eiderdown, piles of linen cushions and oversized feather bolsters make it particularly inviting. On the floor, faded rugs provide warmth and soften the room.

have adapted their style to suit their new surroundings. Amanda describes the look as 'simple and white, with pretty vintage finds.' The styling is creative and the subtle colour palette complements the views of the garden.

The house had previously been used as a weekend cottage so the kitchen was in need of a little updating. Amanda wanted something 'simple and unfussy that looked as if it had always been there'. The cabinets were handmade in the British Standard workshop, just up the road, while the worktops were created by a local craftsman from reclaimed scaffolding boards. The new elements work perfectly with the original brick floor and the existing Rayburn range cooker.

The next project will be to extend Belle's studio in the garden. A talented photographer with a distinctive style, Belle spends her days pursuing photography full time, hosting workshops at the Country Brocante fairs and creating her own prints and postcards.

A quirky feature of the cottage is that each bedroom has its own tiny narrow staircase. These lead to small rooms with pitched, beamed ceilings and low windows dressed with white voile curtains. The beds are particularly inviting – made up in layers of pastel bed linen and topped with lace or floral bedspreads and the softest frilled cushions. There is a multitude of different influences in this house, from Rachel Ashwell to Cabbages & Roses, and Amanda and Belle tie them all together seamlessly with their vintage pieces, original artwork and shared love of all things old, timeworn and faded.

OPPOSITE An oversized crinoline lampshade hangs from the eaves in Belle's pretty attic bedroom. Her bed is dressed with layers of feminine lace and frilled linen. Unframed watercolours are stuck to the wall above the low window and a tiny jug of flowers looks sweet perched upon a chunky beam.

ABOVE A corner of the eaves is home to a lovely collection of vintage baskets and straw hats. Collected over many years from fairs and markets, each one holds a special memory. The natural hues of the straw complement the rich tones of the wood.

RIGHT AND FAR RIGHT On one side of the bed, a wooden chest still has its original sugared-almond pink paint. On the other side, on Belle's bedside table, an unusual French antique lamp decorated with crystal and brass flowers still sports its original ruched silk shade.

OPPOSITE The kitchen table is an ideal place for Caroline to work on her embroidery designs, as it is flooded with natural light from the doorway that leads to the beautiful courtyard. The walls are panelled from floor to ceiling in simple tongue and groove and painted softest dove grey. The pigeonhole shelving holds a collection of vintage stoneware pots.

RIGHT In the small kitchen, fitted cupboards are a simple backdrop for pieces of white French china, which look striking against the dark grey walls. An old French sign hangs above the butler sink and adds to the character of the room.

A STITCH IN TIME
Embroiderer and designer Caroline Zoob has been a great inspiration and support to me over the years. A woman of many talents and skills, she has the most exquisite eye and her beautiful, detailed embroideries are testament to this. Caroline is a leader in her field – an inspirational personality who shares her skills with others, she has built a wonderful career through her design work.

LEFT The living room boasts an abundance of deep neutrals, which give a pleasing visual depth and warmth to the space. The rich patina of the vintage wooden drawer unit is picked up in the collection of decorative pieces and paintings above.

OPPOSITE Again, Caroline plays with light and dark tones. Walls are painted in a pale shade inspired by her collection of old stoneware, and natural light from the window is reflected in the mirrored window frames above the sofa. Richness is introduced via the charcoal velvet cushions and grey throw on the sofa and, especially, the stunning painting of hydrangeas, which served as inspiration for the colour palette here.

For over a decade, Caroline and her husband Jonathan were custodian tenants of Monk's House, the cottage in Rodmell, Sussex, where Leonard and Virginia Woolf made their home for more than fifty years. In particular, they were responsible for restoring and maintaining the extraordinary garden. It was extremely rewarding but very hard work, so after ten years they were ready to downsize and create their own home and garden. They decided to look for somewhere simpler and smaller that had not been tinkered with and a blank canvas of a garden.

The couple now live in Burwash, a pretty village famous for its pollarded lime trees flanking a high street of weatherboarded cottages and rather grander mansions with views across the Sussex Weald to Bateman's, once

the home of writer Rudyard Kipling. Their home is a modest brick-built Edwardian cottage in a row of eight pairs, built along the top of a bank at the edge of the village.

On moving to Burwash, Caroline and Jonathan's priority was to create a vegetable garden with raised beds surrounded by espaliered apple trees and two plum trees. The area outside the living room has been laid with reclaimed York stone and now houses Caroline's collection of vintage gardenalia.

The house is very plain – a no-frills cottage designed and built for farm workers on nearby estates – and any period features had been torn out in the 1980s. Caroline remembers that at one point during the renovation she could see the sky from the ground floor as the house had been stripped right back to its skeleton. Caroline wanted to keep the house simple and spare to disguise its small proportions., so just before moving, the couple commissioned a new building in

the garden to hold Jonathan's grand piano and their collection of books. Now smothered in roses and clematis, the garden room is one of Caroline's favourite parts of the house.

The chief challenges were the small size of the house, a complete lack of storage and the scarcity of any interesting or characterful features. Although Caroline took the opportunity to declutter when they moved, storage was needed throughout the house. In meeting all of these challenges she has been helped incalculably by John Taylor of Woodpigeon (see pages 128–137 for John's own home), an antiques dealer with an exceptional eye. He designed cupboards with doors that give the effect of a panelled wall, tucking them into alcoves and under eaves, fitting reclaimed doors in some places and finishing everything with his proprietary paint finish. John also installed panelling in the entrance hall and main bedroom, adding personality and warmth to the rooms.

OPPOSITE There are so many wonderful textures here, from the layers of old paintwork on the large metal lantern in the fireplace to the natural fibres of the sisal rug and the slubby French linen laid over the armchair.

ABOVE LEFT TO RIGHT Caroline has a knack for charming decorative details. A cluster of stoneware pots supports a time-worn letter; a cherished wooden decoy duck sits on a set of painted drawers; the colours of the painting over the fireplace draw out subtle green undertones in the decorative houses.

The living room was created by knocking down a wall between two smaller rooms. The east-west light in the house suits Caroline's chosen palette of warm greys, which includes a dark grey painted floor and reclaimed slate in the kitchen. One of the first things Caroline bought for the house was a beautiful half-glazed door in its original grey paint, and for this John Taylor created an enormous carcass, providing plentiful storage. Indeed, most of the furniture in the house was sourced from or painted by Woodpigeon. Caroline loves collecting paintings, and they are often the starting point for her rooms. A striking oil painting of hydrangeas from Rosehip in the Country (see page 78–91) suggested the paint colours in the living room.

Caroline is gentle in her approach, and you can see this in her interiors – everything feels calm and effortless. As with her work, the colours are perfectly balanced, the soft grey walls harmonize with the raw linens and natural tones in the paintings. Caroline has a love of French finds and much of the furniture, textiles and artworks were purchased from French dealers. However, she also has a fondness for the traditional English look, which is apparent throughout her home and garden.

ABOVE An alcove in the bedroom holds a chest of drawers with two large candlesticks set either side of an old painted mirror. Silver and glass trinket pots and photo frames are accompanied by a vase of garden flowers that add a touch of colour.

RIGHT A necklace of delicate seed pearls and vintage lilac ribbon spills out of a silver dish on Caroline's dressing table.

FAR RIGHT Antique French nightgowns with exquisite, finely detailed embroidery hang on the back of the bedroom door.

THIS PAGE Pale grey wooden panelling provides a backdrop in the main bedroom. The bed is dressed in white bedlinen with floral pillowcases. The small room is dominated by the large French mirror just seen to the left, which has beautiful foxing and is the standout piece in this room.

OPPOSITE The graceful sweep of the staircase greets visitors as they step through the front door to Lou and Jon's home. The hallway walls are painted in Farrow & Ball's Pavilion Grey and light floods in from the wide door that leads to the courtyard, washing over the bleached wooden floorboards. The charcoal-grey wool stair runner and sisal rug introduce a more contemporary mood.

RIGHT A view across the hallway highlights the beautiful Victorian newel post and curving handrail. The rich tones of the polished wood gleam against the muted neutral paintwork.

TONES AND TEXTURES I first met Lou Bunning

and her husband Jon many years ago, while I was working in a friend's shop. Prior to opening her shop Mora Lifestyle in Norwich, Lou exhibited with us at The Country Brocante. Her talent for interiors and Jon's expertise in developing properties make them a design dream team.

Lou and Jon spent many years living in West Sussex, working on a large renovation project, but once this was completed, they decided they would like to move back to Norfolk. 'We know the county so well, having previously lived on the Norfolk coast for ten years,' explains Lou, 'We always saw ourselves moving back to this part of the country one day.'

After viewing several rural houses, all of which felt too isolated, they concluded that a more urban setting would suit them better. They were lucky enough to view their house just before it went on the open market and instantly fell in love with the ornate ceilings, bleached wooden floorboards and large sash windows. 'As soon as we walked in, we both knew it was the one for us,' recounts Lou.

THIS PAGE The kitchen is a dramatic space, with its austere granite countertops and open shelving. Every surface is accessorized with Lou's treasures – stoneware and silver-plated punchbowls and compotes add vintage elements to the monochrome colour scheme. The *Boulangerie* sign adds a quirky graphic touch.

The house is Grade II listed and was built in 1869 by local architect Edward Boardman in a quiet location within easy walking distance of Norwich town centre. It is a striking yellow brick property, part of a terrace of seven double-fronted houses close to the green space of the Plantation Garden.

It's no exaggeration to say that the house is breathtaking. On entering the hall, Lou's signature style is immediately apparent – lots of natural materials and textures. There is a wonderful sweeping staircase and huge windows, which offer glimpses of the paved courtyard garden. Thanks to years of collecting and time spent living in France, Lou has slowly amassed a fabulous array of antiques and textiles, all of which are displayed to perfection in the large Victorian property. The contrasting textures and natural tones work so well alongside the original features of the house. Many of the elements in this home are simple, even earthy, with inspiration clearly drawn from nature, yet they are woven together so skilfully that the overall effect is one of simple elegance. The house boasts many enviable features – high ceilings, graceful plasterwork and huge windows that flood the space with light – and the Victorian architectural details provide the perfect backdrop for Lou and Jon's treasures.

The previous owners had done an excellent job of renovating the house, installing an incredible lighting system, underfloor heating, high-spec bathrooms and a huge Aga range cooker in the stunning kitchen. 'All the improvements were ones we would have done ourselves,' explains Lou, 'so we were really pleased to have found a property where all the hard work had already been done.' With much of the renovation complete, Lou set to work to put her own stamp on the house, introducing her favoured palette of warm, earthy shades, then dressing the rooms with much-loved decorative pieces.

BELOW LEFT This primitive old metal dipper makes a quirky home for a block of French kitchen soap and brushes.

BELOW CENTRE A set of antique drawers with only the faintest wash of their original paint remaining hangs on the wall of the utility room and holds the laundry supplies.

BELOW A wooden grain scoop with a gorgeous weathered patina has been cleverly repurposed as a wall cabinet and towel rail.

THIS PAGE Antique finds have been put into use in the utility room. An old set of drawers with chipped paint contains laundry essentials while the wirework basket and wooden bowl provide storage for linen.

THIS PAGE This tranquil corner is a masterclass in using natural tones to bring warmth and interest to a space. The collection of wood and stone pieces at the end of the marble mantelpiece echo the faded sepia hue of the handsome wooden cabinet.

The sitting room plays host to the most spectacular floor-to-ceiling gilt mirror that entirely occupies one wall and originally came from the Louvre in Paris. Linen armchairs dressed with faded floral cushions sit alongside antique furniture. When sourcing, Lou seems to have a knack for discovering items that retain their original paint or boast particularly attractive graining or patina, and it is these pieces that are at the heart of her interior style.

Moving through the house, you experience many contrasting textures, both rough and smooth, from natural objects such as dried seedheads to cool marble to sumptuous raw silk. Antique textiles and faded wood are everywhere. The house is coolly formal and wonderfully opulent, yet still manages to feel warm and homely.

Lou's store Mora Lifestyle is located a five-minute walk away in Norwich's Upper St Giles Street and is a wonderful place to glean inspiration for her look. Lou stocks clothing and artisan homewares in her signature colour palette. Also included is a selection of the vintage wares and decorative antiques that create her unique Country Brocante style.

ABOVE In the home office, a decorative deskscape sits against creamy walls. A row of assorted vintage finds is part-display, part-storage. The sombre hues chime with those of the seascape above.

FAR LEFT Rich in textures, Lou's home is a feast for the senses as well as the eyes. On show here are a vintage linen cushion with a pompom trim and a piece of antique broderie anglaise in a dusky taupe shade.

LEFT A battered but beautiful clay pot with its incised pattern all but worn away is the perfect companion for this wooden cabinet.

BELOW Lou's shop, Mora Lifestyle, is every bit as beautiful as you'd expect. Here, handcrafted wares and beautiful clothing sit alongside her vintage finds. On one wall, a rustic shelf holds a collection of autumnal shades, from the burnt orange of the pot and the dried hydrangeas, to the faded straw of the hat and bag.

RIGHT AND OPPOSITE Again in the shop, a large pigeonhole shelving unit is placed on a desk and is used to display various earthenware cups with a beautiful pale blue glaze. The colours pick up on the lovely deep blue of the window display and shuttering.

BELOW RIGHT Dappled sunlight falls on a pile of natural linen fabric displayed on a simple country stool, its great age evident from myriad cracks in the wood.

GATHERINGS   FLORA SHEDDEN

HANS BLOMQUIST   IN DETAIL

FERNANDEZ & WELLS

RU

THE NATURAL HOME.   HANS BLOMQUIST

a life less ordinary

OPPOSITE The porch and hallway are floored with reclaimed bricks. The old French bench, which still retains some of its original paint, is heaped with soft cushions covered in antique linen and faded florals. A heavy curtain keeps out any winter draughts.

RIGHT A painted buffet in the kitchen holds the treasured pottery, both French and English, that Jenny has collected on her travels. The rest of the kitchen has been kept deliberately simple and clutter free, allowing the buffet, with its intriguing patina of peeling paint, to take centre stage.

ENTENTE CORDIALE Deep in rural Suffolk, Nine

Elms Farm perfectly embodies the Country Brocante look. Here, Jenny and Simon Nicole and their daughter Kate have effortlessly combined two very different styles to create a happy marriage of quintessentially English architecture and typically French textiles and antiques.

LEFT In the kitchen, an antique lace panel found at a French market has been transformed into a curtain, cleverly hiding the refrigerator and other mundane items Jenny would prefer not to have on show.

ABOVE AND OPPOSITE Jenny describes the kitchen as 'mainly traditional, with a long French plank table to eat and prepare food on.' The kitchen sink has been cleverly positioned in front of the window to give the washer-upper a glorious outlook. I would be more than happy doing the dishes here, as the garden boasts roses, a stunning lawn and views across farmland.

Jenny and Simon divide their time between Suffolk and France, where they source textiles and furniture for their company Rosehip in the Country, which also sells Jenny's delicate handmade creations. Their daughter Kate has followed in their footsteps and started up her own business, Oyster Bridge & Co, for which she produces beautiful paper treasures adorned with exquisite calligraphy, painted artwork and hand-sewn details. The Nicoles' boundless creativity is what first brought us together. Upon meeting them at another fair, I set

about wooing them until I managed to persuade them to come and be part of our Country Brocante event. As a family, what they create is truly wonderful.

Their home, built in 1640, is a perfect example of a traditional Suffolk farmhouse, also known as a long house. It has a thatched roof and is timber framed, which affords the house much character thanks to the sturdy wooden beams that adorn the internal walls and ceilings. While the house is Suffolk through and through, the interior reveals a strong French influence. In every room, brick, stone and

THIS PAGE This striking room is framed by original beams and dressed to perfection with Jenny's decorative and brocante finds. The sofas are covered in monogrammed French linen sheets and dressed with fabulous cushions and antique quilts. The unusual wirework lampshade was made by Jenny many years ago – she likes to hang trinkets and treasures from it.

rustic weathered wood is combined with an abundance of beautiful vintage fabrics and textiles.

Jenny and Kate have worked hard to create an interior that's in harmony with the history and atmosphere of this beautiful old building. The timber framing has been left exposed and is very much part of the decor. The wooden beams and the stone floors provide a canvas onto which the family has projected their own creative personalities.

Despite the low ceilings, there is a great feeling of light and space here – the off-white walls and the soft tones in the flooring seem to bounce the daylight around.

At the heart of the home is a large room that serves as a studio space for Jenny and Kate. A huge worktable is covered with baskets brimming with lace trim, linen fragments and buttons. Those with a passion for fabrics would find it hard to resist a rummage though an old

OPPOSITE A beautiful old brick wall provides a stunning backdrop to the workroom. The functional workbench, made from timeworn wood panels, holds baskets and crates filled with fabric remnants and trims. A French armchair reupholstered in soft washed linen offers a comfy respite from the worktable.

RIGHT Each room flows perfectly into the next, linked by the restful colour palette. The bleached beams, natural brick floors and pale walls reflect the light, lending an airy and spacious feel to the farmhouse interior.

LEFT A Hungarian trestle bench supports treasured artwork by Jenny's daughter Kate, who is renowned for her intricate and delicate hand-sewn and painted artworks. These are special pieces that will never be sold.

OPPOSITE AND BELOW The workroom is the busy hub of the house. Jenny spends much of her time in here, creating new pieces, sewing and working alongside daughter Kate. The focal point is a generous work table made by husband Simon from large wooden boards set upon oak trestles, providing Jenny and Kate with space to give their creativity free rein.

painted armoire piled high with French linens in delicious pastel shades and faded florals, many of which retain their original mends and fixes. The mood here is one of creative chaos, due to the assortment of textiles and the abundance of pieces awaiting use, but there is also clarity and a sense of calm. This is where Jenny produces her collection of linen dresses, bags and other handmade pieces, which she sells alongside antique and vintage finds. Packages are wrapped in tissue paper and carefully tied with vintage ribbon then set to one side, ready to post.

Wandering the house, I discover a particularly beautiful room with the original plaster still on the walls and faded green oak

THIS PAGE In the main bedroom, freshly laundered linen dresses the upholstered wooden bed. The charcoal-striped duvet cover strikes a crisp masculine note in this graceful space and is perfectly complemented by the pale walls and handmade floral blinds. An old painted cupboard is just the right height to act as a bedside table/nightstand and holds an oil painting of a dramatic landscape.

window frames. This room embodies the use of raw textures in the house and the way in which they work so harmoniously with the contents. Drawn in by the collection of beautiful objects, I'm told this space is a stockroom for finished pieces. The space is a collector's dream, filled with an assortment of mirrors, boxes of china and rails of linen garments.

The house seems to go on and on, each room testament to the Nicoles' unerring sense of style. In one corner of the kitchen, ancient wooden stairs climb to a secret room – the steepest staircase I have ever come across, only to be attempted at the climber's risk. It leads to a cosy little room with wonky ceiling beams, home to Jenny's collection of vintage quilts. The simple decor offers a contrast to the richness of the fabrics and showcases the textiles to perfection.

Many people who run a business from home create a divide between work and family life. But here the owners' passion for what what they do is evident in every room. The very building in which they live and the beautiful finds with which they surround themselves are an everyday inspiration.

ABOVE LEFT The wonky landing walls double as a gallery space, showcasing Jenny and Simon's collection of antique and vintage paintings – rural landscapes interspersed with floral oil paintings.

ABOVE RIGHT The spare bedroom is simple and minimal. The beautiful old metal bed is made up with striped linen that tones perfectly with the Roman blind, while the walls are painted a soft bluish-grey that's conducive to a restful night's sleep.

THIS PAGE The bedroom above the kitchen can be accessed up the main stairs and along the landing or via a steep staircase tucked away behind the kitchen door. The small plank door retains its original floral paper and paint, found when they bought the house, and the bed is covered in antique quilts.

OPPOSITE The bathroom has bare boards and a roll-top tub and is simply furnished with a small armoire that holds toiletries and a shelf for a mirror, pictures and bottles.

LEFT The view from the kitchen through to the sitting room. Floppy linen cushions on the large white sofa complete the relaxed look and the antique crystal and brass chandelier displayed on the sideboard brings a touch of elegance. The faded rug contributes gentle pastel tones.

OPPOSITE An arrangement of favourite vintage finds adds interest to a corner of the kitchen. Bleached wooden boards and a tiny zinc tub hang from hooks above a set of French enamel jars. Beyond can be seen the wood-burning stove and a vintage enamel coal scuttle.

SHABBY MEETS COUNTRY Steph Eley

and I were introduced by a mutual friend, but I knew of her long before we met as I had heard of the wonderful sales she held. Steph did not sell through the internet and this gave her an almost mythical status among buyers. Luckily, I was able to persuade her to bring her trademark painted furniture, linen accessories and decorative treasures to the Country Brocante fair.

OPPOSITE Simple, traditional cabinets with a pale grey countertop create a division between the cooking and dining areas in the kitchen. The soft chalky palette unifies the contrasting textures of the brick fireplace and painted cupboard.

RIGHT A view past an old chair with handmade French linen covers to the sunny porch area beyond. There, a linen curtain conceals storage for everyday necessities and the warm tones of a large French shopping basket echo the wooden beam above the window.

Steph's home is nestled in the high street of a pretty Oxfordshire village. She lives with her partner and a whole host of animals in a honey-coloured Hornton stone cottage, a former bakery and butcher's shop dating back to 1747. The couple moved here to be closer to family and undertook a total renovation inside and out, doing most of the work themselves. Steph describes her style as shabby chic inspired with a dash of French country, and the interior is white, light and bright throughout.

The cottage is entered through a gate into a pretty courtyard garden that leads into an open-plan kitchen with a large wood burner at one end and an old cream Aga at the other. This room is filled with beautiful white-painted cupboards and cabinets, one of which houses Steph's collection of old French terrines. There is a large rustic kitchen table, and comfortable armchairs and dog beds – plenty of room for everyone. The kitchen feels ready to welcome family and friends, even those in muddy boots!

THIS PAGE An Aga range cooker is set into the old chimneyplace and surrounded by country kitchen essentials such as the stovetop kettle and Aga toasting rack. The warm-toned metal pendants add character and visual interest as well as excellent task light.

RIGHT A handsome old oil painting with an ornate gilt frame hangs on the attic stairs, providing a dramatic contrast to the all-white decor.

FAR RIGHT A wrought-iron garden chair is repurposed as a characterful bedside table/nightstand and topped with vintage books in pastel shades.

BELOW A tiny glass chandelier hangs above a guest bed. The washed linen sheets and frilled pillowcases give the bed a relaxed feminine appeal.

Steph and her family enjoy an outdoor country life and although she has gone for a very clean white look in her home, the interior is both pretty and practical. All the soft furnishings have white linen covers that can be taken off and thrown in the washing machine whenever necessary.

Adjoining the kitchen is a comfortable sitting room dominated by a huge, squashy, white corner sofa. This space is home to some delightful pieces, including a pair of old French shutters with their original paint, now peeling attractively, a large mirrored armoire, antique chandeliers and a white enamelled stove. The bay window is a recent addition and overlooks the courtyard garden.

Upstairs, three double bedrooms showcase Steph's style beautifully. All the rooms are painted white but lifted with subtle touches of colour. The overall look is feminine and French, thanks to the monogrammed French linen and lace panels that adorn the windows and the frilled white bedding. Although the rooms are simply furnished, each contains one statement piece. The master bedroom has a magnificent French cane bed, with the rich tobacco colour of the caning picked up in a lavish gilt mirror hanging above. The bedrooms are filled with tiny decorative details

THIS PAGE This cosy attic bedroom, with its double bed tucked away under the eaves, is warmed by a tiny white enamel stove. The large square pillows are covered in blue Catherine Rose pillowcases from Cabbages & Roses.

– a floral teacup on a bedside table, vases of flowers and dainty crystal chandeliers. Vintage French metal chairs, painted white armoires and old chests of drawers give the room a faded elegance.

I was instantly drawn to Steph's sewing room at one of the converted attic – a heavenly little space that's straight out of a children's story book. The attic is accessed via a reclaimed Victorian staircase and is a cosy hideaway filled with the textiles, lace and trims used to create Steph's much-coveted chairs, cushions and accessories. At the other end of the attic is a tiny bedroom, dressed in white cotton and linen. A slouchy armchair and simple decorative details keep this space true to Steph's style.

OPPOSITE Country charm gives way to sophisticated elegance in the master bedroom. The antique French cane bed, a rare and fortuitous find, is beautifully dressed in layers of white linen, affording the bed a sumptuous feel.

ABOVE A vintage armchair has some of its original hessian/burlap scrim visible, which contrasts with the white linen to striking effect. The large window is screened with simple white voile and a panel of pale floral linen fabric.

RIGHT A zinc tub of pink roses decorates the chest of drawers in the bedroom. Just visible at the top of the wall is old Cabbages & Roses wallpaper in the raspberry Hatley print that has been lightly whitewashed over, creating a faded, chalky version of an old favourite.

THIS PAGE The central space in the renovated attic is home to an old painted wrought-iron cot piled high with cushions and vintage linens. Exposed beams and brickwork reveal the framework of the house and the personality of the building. The low door to Steph's sewing room gives the attic an *Alice in Wonderland* feel.

ABOVE The work surface in Steph's sewing room is crowded with needles, threads and scraps of antique fabric. Enamel jars and a set of painted drawers provide storage for sewing essentials.

RIGHT Hanging on one of the attic walls, this lovely old coat rack displays a vintage French nightshirt and a tiny zinc bucket holding dried flowers.

Like many of us who obsess over our interiors, Steph's home is constantly changing. Furniture is moved around, and, as with all dealers, things come and go, making room for new pieces. Steph is quite fearless – she tells stories of knocking down walls or windows on a whim then, quite by chance, finding a window frame in a skip/dumpster or at a barn sale that perfectly fits the empty space.

Steph took us to visit her 'homestead', where her daughter's horse and their other animals live. A converted barn, it not only provides extra living space but also functions as both a stockroom and showroom. Seemingly effortlessly, Steph has struck an enviable life-work balance. She combines country life with her business, Pearly Hill, sourcing and selling decorative antiques and, along the way, she has created an elegant and refined home.

OPPOSITE The far end of Steph's barn storeroom is home to a tiny kitchen area, complete with a gas hob/stovetop. A large enamel bowl acts as a makeshift sink. Vintage finds, such as the Victorian baby's bath and the set of antlers, lend a stylish air to what would otherwise be a utilitarian space.

LEFT AND BELOW LEFT The barn acts as a showroom for Steph's antiques business Pearly Hill and is beautifully arranged and accessorized as you would expect. French enamel jars and antique lamps sit on top of a painted chest of drawers with an arched overmantel mirror propped on top (left) while windfalls from the garden are gathered in an enamel bowl (below left).

BELOW An old horse box has been converted into a cosy nook from which Steph can enjoy her 'homestead'. A simple wooden bench covered in a vintage eiderdown and cushions creates a comfortable day bed while the garden table and chair set provides the perfect place for a cup of tea.

LEFT Sophie's hallway welcomes visitors into the cottage – a perfectly placed jug/pitcher filled with wild flowers bringing a hint of colour and English-country-cottage charm to what is essentially a French-inspired space.

OPPOSITE A traditional clothes airer, or Sheila Maid, hangs above the Aga range cooker. A selection of Iris Handverk brushes hang from a Shaker peg rail. Vintage Swedish dishes are stored in a small painted plate rack found at a fair, with a collection of Caroline Zoob bowls above.

SIMPLE LUXURY
Sophie Bateman is a friend and a regular at the Country Brocante fairs. We have a shared love of homemaking and bonded over piles of folded linen and vintage Cabbages & Roses prints. A classically trained singer, Sophie also has a degree in art and design and a talent for styling. Her home is an expression of this. Everything has been thoughtfully considered, from fabrics and colours to paintings and decorative objects.

OPPOSITE The long, narrow Scandinavian fruitwood kitchen table is a good fit for the small kitchen. The blind is made from Kate Forman's Kitty fabric. A collection of white French enamel pieces creates a simple display on the windowsill.

RIGHT Pastel-toned Kate Forman cushions dress the linen-upholstered sofas in the sitting room. The walls are painted in Farrow & Ball's Great White and hung with prints found at brocante fairs along with paintings by local artists. The pretty painted corner cabinet holds a collection of Victorian glass bottles.

Sophie lives with her husband and three of their five children in a small Victorian farmworker's cottage on the edge of West Sussex. Their home is in an idyllic spot overlooked by the South Downs, framed by blossom trees and tucked neatly into the bend of a river. An old brick path leads through the pretty garden to a tiled porch. Everything speaks of quintessential country charm, yet on stepping inside there is a different twist on the classic cosy cottage style; the interior is light, airy, calm and elegant.

The family previously lived in a spacious Georgian house but this dream home became a nightmare of dry rot and deathwatch beetle. With dwindling funds and the financial crash looming they downsized to the cottage, which became a place of much-needed peace and security.

I can detect a Georgian influence in Sophie's home – it is ordered, harmonious and elegant. The interior is also fresh and bright, with an impression of space achieved by a subtle palette, lots of mirrors to reflect the light and,

above all, simplicity. 'Simplicity enables us to live here with a large family, We had to rethink how we lived in this space. We had to reduce our possessions and pare everything back, but without compromising on beauty or comfort.' Sophie explains.

Furniture has been kept to a minimum and storage has been carefully chosen. Painted cupboards, baskets and enamel jars hold the inevitable clutter of family life, keeping surfaces clear. 'I love the William Morris adage of keeping only what one knows to be useful or believe to be beautiful,' says Sophie. 'So, for example, in the kitchen we only have space for our favourite items, but this does mean that we use and enjoy the things we love most every day.'

The Aga range cooker is the heart of the kitchen, while in the sitting room a cream enamel wood burner offers a comforting focal point. 'We have no need for central heating as the two heat the cottage perfectly, but in this respect we do live a rather *Little House on the Prairie* existence as, on a cold winter morning, lighting the wood stove is the first and most important job of the day.'

The garden provides additional living space in summer. The back door leads out of the kitchen into a classic cottage garden made up of three distinct 'rooms' divided by hedging and paths, and this mirrors the order and neatness within the house. Beyond the

ABOVE AND LEFT
The Victorian mirror over the fireplace helps create the illusion of more space. A fireguard from Garden Requisites in Bath protects little fingers from the cream enamel Franco Belge wood-burning stove. On the wall, an antique French sconce bears a handmade label from Rosehip in the Country.

OPPOSITE Generous sofas covered in French bedspreads create a comfortable space for all the family. A small footstool spread with Cabbages & Roses fabric doubles up as a place for a tea tray. An 18th-century Russian icon hung in the corner of the room is a unique personal feature.

ABOVE AND ABOVE RIGHT
Below the stairs, woven baskets holding everyday necessities sit on top of a painted cabinet, which is used for storing children's shoes. The painted staircase with stripped wooden treads winds up to the narrow upstairs landing where an unusual Victorian floral mirror hangs above an old half-moon table – a perfect spot to sort fresh laundry.

post-and-rail boundary fence lies grazing pasture that leads down to the river. 'The countryside and the views across the river are magical and are the most special aspect of living here,' Sophie says. 'In the field is a beautiful oak tree, behind which the sun sets, and some of our happiest times are spent looking out, cup of tea in hand, watching the cows make their way across the river, swallows in the sky and the light changing in the early evening.'

Beyond a small picket-fenced kitchen garden stands a traditional shepherd's hut, decorated in the same soothing tones as the house. Cosy and intimate with a tiny wood stove, it is also light and pretty. Sophie explains, 'My hut is my greatest luxury and possibly the one thing in my life I have been really selfish about. It is my sanctuary. I can shut myself away and focus on music or write or just have time to myself. My children are sweetly respectful of this space and always knock!'

THIS PAGE A large Victorian brass bed, made up with white linen and a Kate Forman pink Sophia bedspead, fills the pretty bedroom. Painted cabinets and vintage prints adorn the walls. The Roman blind is made from Kate Forman Sophia in grey and the Edwardian frosted opaline glass pendant light creates a lovely centrepiece.

THIS PAGE In comparison with the muted shades elsewhere, the nursery sings with colour. The walls are Farrow & Ball's Setting Plaster with the panelling picked out in Dix Blue – a warm and inviting combination. An old nursing chair covered in a leaf-print fabric is home to a friendly collection of old bears and stuffed animals.

I love the contradiction of Sophie's home and lifestyle. She lives a bucolic, almost old-fashioned existence in her cottage, yet her home is quite luxurious. There is a formality and elegance to the house, a beautiful visual flow – nothing jars or disturbs the eye. Colours, while muted, are soft and warm. There is a sense of calm and order, neatness and structure, without any stiffness or constraint. Sophie is an idealist at heart and the cottage reflects her desire to live a rural life surrounded by beauty; a cottage lifestyle with all the charms of domesticity, yet without compromising on comfort and elegance.

ABOVE LEFT A procession of vintage German tin animals and figures parade around the top of the wooden panelling.

LEFT A beautiful polished wood table is an unusually grown-up addition to the nursery and lends a touch of elegance to the room. An array of traditional wooden toys sit on top of the large painted chest of drawers.

ABOVE The bathroom is decorated in Farrow & Ball's Ammonite and Wevet, which create a light, fresh feel. A small painted cupboard from a brocante fair introduces vintage detailing, as do the tiny antique porcelain pots that hold bathroom accoutrements.

LEFT Sophie's traditional shepherd's hut was built by Roundhill Shepherd Huts. It is clad with painted corrugated iron and sits on a solid wooden base with huge cast-iron wheels. Wooden steps lead up to the reclaimed stable door and the pane of Victorian stained glass in the door floods the hut with coloured light when caught by the sun.

OPPOSITE The interior of the shepherd's hut has a similar feel to the cottage – light and pretty with feminine touches, such as the French sofa adorned with a vintage quilt. The panelling is painted in Great White by Farrow & Ball and the reclaimed wooden floorboards have been given a light whitewash. A glazed cupboard holds music, books and stationery.

RIGHT The fold-down table was crafted from reclaimed wood and given pretty curved legs, repurposed from Swedish banisters. The Jotul wood stove creates a cosy corner. Above the door sits a gilded wooden shell pelmet, while around the room original prints and decorative antiques add charm and interest.

OPPOSITE Soft warm greys set the tone for Susannah's sleek kitchen. Traditional-style cabinets are topped with dark granite, which introduces a more contemporary touch. Both the sink and the Aga are positioned beneath windows, so whether cooking or washing up the family are able to enjoy beautiful views of the garden. Simple modern shelves display white china and small silver items alongside wooden spoons and rustic pottery.

RIGHT The central hallway is flooded with light from a huge window. Wooden flooring gives way to natural sisal on the stairs. To the left of the staircase is the doorway to the family sitting room, which allows us a glimpse of the warm tones and textures of the soft furnishings.

A SENSE OF CALM Susannah Adorian and I are

friends as well as neighbours; she lives at the other end of a long winding lane from me.

I can't remember now whether our paths first crossed because we lived in the same village,

or because of the Country Brocante fairs, but it was bound to happen eventually as we

share a deep love of France and a passion for interiors.

Susannah, her husband Mark and their two teenage sons recently returned to England after living in the south of France for six years. They still have a house in the Luberon, which they visit regularly, but they felt that with the boys growing up it was time to be closer to family and return to their roots in rural West Sussex.

Their house was originally a sixteenth-century brick and tile-hung cottage, but twentieth-century additions have created a handsome and generous family home. It stands in beautiful grounds with many features, including a traditional kitchen garden and a ha-ha. There is even a pool and a wooden pool house with an open log fire that's used by the family as an outside dining and entertaining space. Various barns and outhouses of differing ages and styles are dotted around the grounds and there is no shortage of lovely views from the house or interesting aspects in the garden.

The house has all the hallmarks of a traditional Sussex farmhouse, complete with diamond-paned lattice windows and ancient oak beams. The beams were originally dark, which gave the house quite a heavy atmosphere, so Susannah had them sandblasted, which, she says, made a huge difference to the feel of the place. The interior was completely redecorated and a new kitchen installed, complete with an Aga range cooker that provides a cosy farmhouse atmosphere. The kitchen is traditional in style while maintaining a clean, uncluttered feel. Dark granite worktops complement the glossy black enamel of the Aga, while the muted tones of the Farrow & Ball-painted cabinets and walls create a calm, restful backdrop. Chunky wall-hung shelving displays some of

ABOVE One end of the dining-room mantelpiece is home to an array of vintage treasures, including an antique horn and a charming gilt-framed print. To the left, you can spy old walking sticks and shepherd's crooks in the entrance hall.

RIGHT AND OPPOSITE Original ceiling beams dominate the dining room. The table is covered with a Cabbages & Roses floral linen and surrounded by painted wooden dining chairs. The feel is almost Gustavian, yet the decorative elements root it firmly in the English style.

THS PAGE The sitting room has a traditional English character. Neutral-toned walls serve as a backdrop for the polished furniture. Long curtains fall to the sisal flooring and sumptuous cushions in a deep pink floral print accessorize the sofa. The layers of different textures, colours and patterns give the room a warm and welcoming feel.

Susannah's beautiful vintage china and small curiosities, and the scrubbed pine kitchen table serves as the centrepiece of the room.

Susannah's taste is impeccable; the house feels sophisticated and stylish yet still retains a relaxed, rural charm. She has chosen an elegant, subdued colour palette and there is an abundance of light despite the low ceilings. Rooms are filled with family heirlooms and pieces from their time in France. 'We wanted to achieve a calm but not overly neutral decoration,' Susannah explains. 'Farrow & Ball paints, sisal carpets and faded curtains and blinds helped achieve this. Lots of finds from France and the UK helped layer up to create a fairly uncluttered but cosy look.'

Textiles and patterns feature throughout the house, including lots of floral linens by Kate Forman and Cabbages & Roses as well as touches of warmth and depth in the form of other fabrics. Despite the graceful decor, it is obviously a relaxed family home where much time is spent hanging out in the drawing room

LEFT A close-up of the mantelpiece shows the distinctive Robert Kime wallpaper on the walls of the snug. A row of books is held in place by an unusual pair of metal bookends embossed with a floral decoration. A tiny vintage toy pig adds an amusing detail.

ABOVE Elegant double doors frame the view from the drawing room to the snug. Just visible in the foreground are the tops of old French pots, part of an impressive collection. In the snug, a large footstool covered in vintage French sack cloth strikes a rustic note in this very civilized room.

and the cosy little snug, which
features a wood-burning stove
and charming small-print
wallpaper by Robert Kime.

Every room in the house has a
breathtaking view of the gardens.
From the window of the snug, for
example, the eye is drawn down
a flight of original stone steps
to the swimming pool then
the fruit trees and finally the
picturesque summerhouse
beyond. Susannah has devoted
much time and thought to the
design and decoration of both
house and garden. The result
is smart and sophisticated yet
comfortable and relaxed, designed
to be lived in and enjoyed –
a dream Sussex farmhouse.

OPPOSITE There is a traditional feel
to this guest bedroom. Twin beds with
simple linen-upholstered headboards
are covered with classic white French
bedspreads. The floral curtains and
cushions complement the dark beams
and bring warmth and character.

RIGHT Upstairs, the original beams
add drama to the simplest spaces,
their warm tones offset beautifully
by the soft, neutral walls. This narrow
corridor is transformed by a pair of
wonderfully luxurious floor-length
Cabbages & Roses French Toile
curtains in deep raspberry.

THIS PAGE With an absence of beams, the main bedroom has a lighter, more spacious feel. The walls are painted in a calming blue-grey that harmonizes with the pastel floral fabrics on the traditional fabric-skirted dressing table, where a collection of vintage silver frames and glass trinket jars sits in front of an antique mirror.

OPPOSITE Fitted cupboards and a panelled bath create a sense of simplicity in the clutter-free bathroom. The large window is dressed with a pretty pink floral blind, which casts a pleasing warm glow into the room. A painted wooden chair and a large porcelain jug are the only decorative details needed.

LEFT Simple pigeonhole shelving houses a museum of curiosities in Barbara Cunnell and John Taylor's sitting room, with the tones of the objects echoing the natural colour palette used throughout the house. Here are Victorian baby shoes, polished skittles, wooden duck decoys and other odds and ends, some valuable and others not, but all valued and brought together to create more than the sum of their parts – the skill of a true collector. These shelves are filled with memories and each item has its own story to tell.

OPPOSITE Outside John's office stands a handsome set of gardener's seed drawers that retain their original paint, handles and lettering. John and Barbara purchased them from Spencer Swaffer Antiques, also in Arundel. Perched on top is an antique French clock made from heavy cast metal that dates from about 1900.

A BIRD IN THE HAND
I first met Barbara Cunnell and John Taylor in the early days of my business and over the years we have become good friends. I have always admired their work and they are still a huge inspiration to me. Trading as Woodpigeon, Barbara and John are very well respected in the trade so having them become part of the Country Brocante elevated us to a new level and was a turning point for the business.

THIS PAGE The dining area is simple and stylish, with dark wood set against clean white walls. The table and chairs are French, while the linen runner is made from an old grain sack and looks beautiful against the polished wood.

Barbara and John both come from a design background and as a couple are renowned for their signature style, which is greatly sought after by a long list of clients. John's ability to restore and design and Barbara's talent for sourcing rare treasures makes them a truly dynamic duo, so seeing what they had achieved with their own home was fascinating.

The couple live in a modern three-storey riverside townhouse on a cobbled street close to the centre of the historic market town of Arundel, West Sussex. Moving in was not without its challenges. The house was very different to the period properties the couple had lived in previously. It had been a rental property, and had what Barbara describes as 'a pretty dismal interior'. Upon taking ownership, the couple 'blitzed it, painting everywhere white so that the spaces revealed themselves to us,' Barbara recalls. 'We have since revisited each room, transforming them to fit our trademark style.' The house now provides a perfect backdrop for Barbara and John's collection of furniture and decorative antiques, with the orderly architecture of the modern building complementing the serene symmetry of their style.

Barbara wanted to create a 'relaxed, calm home' so opted for a limited colour scheme of grey and white tones on both walls and furniture, while the natural finishes and aged patina of the couple's decorative antiques and timeworn treasures contributes an additional palette of subtle and faded tones.

TOP RIGHT A shelf in the kitchen plays host to an array of vintage stoneware and other kitchenalia. Barbara sticks to a restricted colour palette but is clever at using contrasting textures to bring interest, depth and definition.

ABOVE Barbara has a knack for a decorative vignette. The pigeonhole shelving in the sitting room is home to this arrangement, which includes a dark wooden vintage hat stand, old brass candlesticks and a metal mug filled with feathers, all overlooked by the enamel 'B' for Barbara.

It is evident that each piece in the house, whether an object, a kitchen fixture or a piece of furniture, has been carefully considered before inclusion. Nothing has been left to chance; decisions about positioning and placement are thoughtful and measured, creating a sense of harmony between an object and its surroundings. As you stroll through the house, light pours in through the large windows, highlighting small vignettes and displays of antique pieces cleverly curated by Barbara. The building may be modern, but the antique French doors, foxed mirrors and decorative pieces look completely at home here.

In the kitchen, a dark feature wall sets off Barbara's collection of white ironstone china to striking effect. Rather than fitting cabinets on the walls, the couple cleverly repurposed scaffolding boards as open shelves and an enormous antique brie board makes a fabulous feature.

LEFT On top of the old English plate-warming cupboard, or Huffer, a beautifully modelled Italian carved wooden hand sourced from Spencer Swaffer Antiques in Arundel has pride of place among a selection of favourite pieces. A framed piece by Caroline Zoob hangs on the wall above.

THIS PAGE In the sitting room, light floods in from the courtyard garden. The walls are white and the furnishings upholstered in natural textiles. I love the architectural form of the branch perched upon the wall light, bringing together all the natural elements in this room.

THIS PAGE In the spare bedroom, a pair of simply dressed single beds takes centre stage. Beneath the sloping eaves, this room is quiet and restful with soft textures and just a few carefully chosen decorative pieces, such as the tiny antique straw hats displayed on the wall beside the dormer window.

The living room is a bright, light space with French doors opening onto a courtyard garden paved in York stone. This room is full of exceptional pieces yet feels pared-back and clutter free. A large antique French wooden table is perfect for relaxed suppers with friends. Natural sisal flooring and linen furnishings soften the space, making it cosy yet functional. Built-in shelves hold an array of Barbara's most-loved possessions, the culmination of a lifetime of collecting, as well as 'special pieces that I am just not ready to sell'. One particular treasure is the old English Huffer, a tin-lined plate-warming cupboard that would originally have been used for warming a dinner service in front of the fire before being carried to the table. 'It did get taken to one of the Country Brocante Fairs with the intention of selling it,' recounts Barbara, 'but I had a last-minute panic and put it back in the van to take home. This is something that I have never regretted – we love it.'

John and Barbara's tranquil, serene aesthetic never falters. This calm and considered interior is a true inspiration for those who live in a modern home yet still wish to collect and enjoy decorative antiques.

FAR LEFT A few quirky vintage objects and a small basket to hold trinkets add interest to the bedside table/nightstand.

LEFT As you climb the stairs to the top floor, you are greeted by a painted shelf unit that holds a collection of antique cut-glass bottles. They look striking against the soft grey wall.

ABOVE In a corner of the bedroom shown opposite, an old French chair has been stripped back to its hessian/burlap scrim and dressed with a piece of washed linen and a handmade monogrammed cushion.

OPPOSITE Barbara describes the office as 'a bright sunny room and a pleasure to spend time in.' A feature wall in Farrow & Ball's Mole's Breath gives the room added depth, and in front of this is an old trestle table used as a desk. A carved woodpigeon takes pride of place.

ABOVE AND RIGHT The bathroom is panelled in tongue and groove painted warm white, providing the backdrop to a whole host of covetable pieces. The 19th-century wooden horse was found at Fontaine Decorative (above). Beneath the sloping roof, a shelf unit holds quirky vintage pieces alongside bathroom essentials (above right). A large metal 'B' looks striking perched above the panelling, while dried seed heads and antique coral introduce natural elements and intriguing textures (right).

LEFT With so many treasures and trinkets to display, shelves are essential in Michelle's home. This vintage example retains its original duck-egg blue paintwork, now slightly chipped, which works perfectly against a wall painted in Farrow & Ball's creamy Pointing. An assortment of jugs and enamelware sit on the shelf alongside other quirky finds.

OPPOSITE In the dining room, the look is informal and pretty. A farmhouse table takes centre stage, laid with freshly laundered Hatley linen from Cabbages & Roses. Mismatched chairs and an old bench piled with floral cushions provide seating. Next to a pile of chopping boards on the table, a Caroline Zoob jug holds pink and white anemones from the garden.

FAMILY FRIENDLY I met my friend Michelle Essam many

years ago at one of our first-ever fairs. We both love vintage textiles, so were often found tripping over each other trying to reach the best finds at fairs and car boot/yard sales. We also once shared a shop…although 'shop' is too grand a description. It was an old cowshed on the Knepp Castle Estate in West Sussex – freezing cold and full of mice, but where my business began.

OPPOSITE I'm struck by how prettily the windows are dressed in Michelle's house. The smaller windows are adorned with remnants of pretty French fabric or English florals, simply tacked in place then tied back with a length of ribbon. Every shelf seems to holds an array of intriguing treasures – old French books bound in antique fabric, piles of vintage fabrics, dainty ceramics and enamelware and jugs of fresh flowers. A child-sized pyjama jacket hangs from one shelf, the pocket holding a tiny knitted bear from Michelle's childhood.

THIS PAGE Every table, sideboard and shelf in this house presents some sort of floral display. I particularly love this old zinc pot – a skip/dumpster find – which holds seasonal blooms from Michelle's garden.

THIS PAGE The kitchen is warm and homely, every surface covered with vintage kitchenalia. Michelle has used an old piece of wood as a splashback, giving the whole sink area a warm, rustic feel. The kitchen cabinets were inherited from the previous owner and freshened up with a coat of white paint.

Michelle's house is first and foremost a family home. As soon as you walk through the door, you can sense that it is filled with life and activity, warmth and love. The family moved from a tiny cottage across the lane to this, the old village post office, which is a much better fit. Everything here speaks of close and creative family life. The walls are adorned with photographs and children's drawings, cards inscribed with loving messages and even tiny drawings and sweet words written directly on the wall. There are strings of tree lights, tins full of biscuits/cookies, baskets overflowing with wellies/gum boots and dogs asleep on the boot-room sofa. It is homely and relaxed and it is evident that happiness and comfort are valued above all else.

The move not only allowed the family more space, but also provided Michelle with additional capacity for her ever-growing collections. The house tells her story, one of years of collecting all things old and beautiful, weathered and worn. There is

an abundance of vintage textiles, each piece haggled over and brought home to be loved and cherished. There are old wooden signs and beautiful doors propped against walls, chipped painted cupboards and tiny treasures, all lovingly sourced over the past 25 years.

What I find so endearing about this house is that nothing is precious. All Michelle's antiques and vintage pieces are kept out for the family to use and enjoy. Vintage quilts cover every bed and pretty china is stacked on shelves. Old pieces of wood, complete with their original paintwork, have been reinvented as shelves or side tables, while vintage ladders hold French linen tea towels/kitchen cloths. Just like its owner, the house is full of charm and humour. I love the decorative vignettes – a washing line of vintage baby clothes is strung across the fireplace, miniature teacups and jugs top the mantelpiece and there are teddy bears and dolls scattered here and there. Upstairs, baby clothes hang over the radiators as if drying, despite the fact the babies are

ABOVE LEFT On the kitchen windowsill, hand-thrown pots and stoneware marmalade pots found over the years at antique fairs and car boot/yard sales are used to hold pencils, flowers and other paraphernalia.

ABOVE CENTRE Eggs from Michelle's beloved chickens are piled in bowls and dishes around the room.

ABOVE RIGHT A quirky collection of wooden spoons are grouped together in an old paint kettle.

ABOVE In the sitting room, an old garden table takes centre stage. Surrounding the table are squashy sofas covered in heavy French linen sheets. Nothing is ironed here – crumpled linen is all part of Michelle's look. Two old barn doors with their original paint stand in the corner. This room is light, airy and full of country charm.

now almost all in their teens! There is a whimsical quality to this house; it is clearly a collector's abode but also functions perfectly as a busy family home.

Michelle has a soft spot for Cabbages & Roses fabrics, which appear throughout the house mixed with antique textiles. In the breakfast room, a beautiful old wooden shelf is stacked right up to the ceiling with French and English floral fabrics. In the sitting room, deep squashy sofas covered in vintage linen sheets and old faded quilts are a perfect spot to curl up in the evening.

I am always struck by how relaxed and contented I feel here, immersed in Michelle's world, drinking tea from a beautiful Caroline Zoob mug or an old French china cup, chatting away in a comfy armchair. I am always interested to see the latest finds – unusual pieces that Michelle can't wait to show me. Like all of us, Michelle leads a busy life, but any free time she has is devoted to her passion –searching markets and car boot/yard sales for yet more treasures. Most of these are destined to be sold, but the really special finds will be kept and loved for ever.

THIS PAGE The main bedroom continues the country-cottage-meets shabby-chic theme. Old doors create a characterful backdrop to the metal bedstead and vintage painted furniture provides all the storage Michelle needs. The bed linen is Cabbages & Roses layered with plump vintage quilts. The Westerleigh sign bears no relevance to the house – Michelle found it at a sale and fell in love with it.

WESTERLEICH

LEFT In the hallway, a soft palette of grey and white complements the Victorian-style floor tiles and creates a light and welcoming mood, while a heavy old French linen sheet hung at the door keeps any draughts at bay.

OPPOSITE The light, airy kitchen features traditional-style wooden cabinets and drawers hand-painted soft grey with pale marble worktops, while an antique wooden pediment frames the range cooker perfectly. Open shelving provides Emma with the opportunity to display a carefully curated collection of her white china plates, jugs and tureens.

COUNTRY IN THE CITY I have known

Emma Gurmin since the early days. My very first business, Village Vintage, which I created with my oldest friend Darcy, was where the Country Brocante began. Emma was one of our first exhibitors and joined us with her business Velvet Ribbon, which she has been running for many years.

THIS PAGE The kitchen extension features large windows and French doors that allow the light to stream in, even in winter. The unusual dining table base was created using salvaged pieces from a Russian church while reclaimed boards form the top. The floral painting provides a gentle pop of colour in this bright, welcoming family space.

ABOVE LEFT An antique metal lavabo or water fountain is fixed to the wall and used to display fresh flowers.

ABOVE CENTRE Part of Emma's large collection of vintage French stoneware, sourced while exploring the brocantes of Provence.

ABOVE RIGHT Pretty blue and white china jugs adorn the kitchen shelves alongside more utilitarian pieces.

OVERLEAF The stunning Swedish Rococo cabinet is the focal point in the kitchen. It was carefully dry-scraped by Emma to reveal its original chalky-white paintwork – a time-consuming technique that was a true labour of love. It opens to reveal shelves that groan under the weight of Emma's treasured jugs, pots and decorative china, alongside pretty candles and antique French boxes with floral fabric covers.

Emma's particular passion is French textiles. She cleverly sources quilts, linens, remnants and pieces of antique and vintage French fabrics, which she sells alongside French decorative furniture and objects. I knew Emma's house would be very white, very pretty and full of very special pieces she can't bear to part with.

The house was built in 1908 and is a classic Victorian terraced yellow-brick cottage. After spending several years living in Hong Kong, Emma and her young family returned to London, where they were keen to put down roots. The house was in desperate need of updating, so Emma and her husband Seb set about opening it up, knocking down walls and adding a family room with a pitched roof at the back of the house. The addition of large sash windows throughout has created a light and airy space with a fresh, contemporary feel that provides the perfect backdrop for Emma's furniture and huge collection of textiles.

The flooring is predominantly pale bleached wood, which works so well with the clean white walls and original painted furniture. The rooms are filled with delicate and pretty French finds, antique armoires and decorative light fittings. Emma has hung old floral paintings on the walls and simple linen drapes and curtains at the windows. It feels pared back and simple, yet there is plenty to entice the eye.

The Swedish Rococo armoire in the dining area is testament to a lifetime spent collecting. Inside, vintage sheets and table linen jostle for space among piles of china and pretty enamelware. The dining table, although found at an antiques fair in the UK, originates from a Russian church roof and dates back to 1780. With its exuberant curves, original blue paint and worn patina, it makes the most stunning

LEFT A collection of framed *herbiers* in whitewashed frames, dating to about 1890, adorn the wall behind the sofa. The hand-carved angel wing would originally have been used as a papier mâché mould.

ABOVE This tiny gilt crown with crystal embellishments would once have adorned a religious statue of a saint. Now it adds sparkle to a corner of Emma's living room.

centrepiece. Although Emma's house has been styled to perfection, it is a family home at heart and the elements of everyday life are evident throughout. Little painted chests of drawers hold colouring pencils for Emma's two daughters, while pretty little bowls and boxes hold their trinkets and toys.

The house feels very feminine and is heavily influenced by Emma's frequent trips to the south of France, a place where she spends much time with her mother, sister and children, combining family holidays with buying expeditions. Emma has a whole host of secret spots for buying fabric, closely guarded connections that she visits

in order to track down the best pieces. When Emma attends the Country Brocante fair, gasps can be heard as trunks and baskets are opened to reveal her newly sourced treasures. In the master bedroom, pile upon pile of quilts are stacked in a pretty armoire, supposedly ready to provide extra warmth on chilly evenings, but really just there to be adored and enjoyed by Emma.

The house is full of artful decorative vignettes – gilt mirror frames are leant against the wall, no longer housing their mirror glass but still decorative in their own right. A passion for florals in all forms is evident in this house, and not just on the textiles – old stoneware marmalade jars

THIS PAGE Glazed cupboards were hand built to fit the alcoves either side of the chimneybreast. A large antique mirror reflects light back into the room, while the linen-covered French sofa invites visitors to sit and chat.

and teacups and jugs hold roses and peonies cut from the garden. The sitting room has a more formal feel. Linen-covered antique sofas, sparking chandeliers and a sprinkling of Swedish pieces make for a glamorous and grown-up space. Particular treasures are kept behind glass cupboard doors. Reclaimed glazed doors have been used to create a divide between the sitting room and dining room, cleverly installed so they can be swung open to create a large open-plan living space when needed.

Emma's house has all the charm of a traditional London Victorian terraced house, but sprinkled throughout is the decorative magic of France.

THIS PAGE The master bedroom is a wonderfully light attic space, created by the couple when the house was extended and providing a restful retreat. Soft linen bedding blends beautifully with Emma's many vintage floral quilts and French doors open on to a Juliet balcony.

LEFT These vintage shelves and the chest of drawers next to them are piled high with pretty fabric remnants. Florals, stripes and checks all sit happily alongside one another and Emma often creates beautiful cushions with the smaller pieces – no scraps are too small to be given a new lease of life.

BELOW LEFT A stack of pretty old frames retaining their original paint provide the perfect opportunity to display delicate pieces of fabric alongside a glass jar full of mother-of-pearl buttons.

BELOW An oversized French carved wood frame surrounds a beautiful and decorative English chest of drawers. The drawers are marked 'South Kensington' inside, giving a clue to where the piece was originally made.

SOURCES

The Country Brocante
Come and meet the merchants and makers at The Country Brocante Fairs, held in spring, summer, autumn and winter. Visit our website for details of the next fair.
www.thecountrybrocante.co.uk
@thecountrybrocante

The Country Brocante Store
Griffin House
West Street
Midhurst GU29 9NQ
Antique and vintage furniture, textiles and decorative details from nine different sellers.

The Country Brocante Meeting House
6 West Street
Midhurst GU29 9NF
+44 (0)1730 810973
The home to Country Brocante Style.

Cowdray Estate
www.cowdray.co.uk
Our summer and winter Country Brocantes are held on the beautiful Cowdray Estate in the South Downs National Park.

Daylesford Organic Farmshop
www.daylesford.com
We hold our Harvest fair at Daylesford Organic Farm in Gloucestershire, alongside their sustainable organic farm and farm shop.

OTHER SOURCES

The Arundel Carpet Company
103–105 Tarrant Street
Arundel
West Sussex BN18 9DP
www.arundelcarpets.co.uk
Natural flooring, wooden floors and traditional carpets.

SJ Bennett Antiques
+44 (0)7879 406843
Decorative homewares plus English and French furniture.

Beyond France
www.beyondfrance.co.uk
Vintage linens from Hungary and handmade cushions and accessories.

British Standard Cupboards
www.britishstandardcupboards.co.uk
Affordable off-the-shelf cabinetry for kitchens and other rooms, handmade in Suffolk.

Blundstone UK
www.blundstone.co.uk
Tasmanian boot company offering tough, comfortable footwear for work and play.

Cabbages & Roses
www.cabbagesandroses.com
A quintessentially British fashion and lifestyle brand with a focus on cosy, generous living. Cabbages & Roses has a slow-fashion ethos and believes in working with local artisans to create everything as locally as possible.

Chalk & Paisley
www.chalkpaisley.bigcartel.com
Unique pieces for the home made from beautiful worn, faded vintage fabrics.

Fabulous Vintage Finds
www.fabulousvintagefinds.co.uk
@fabulousvintagefinds
French decorative antiques, original painted furniture, rustic ceramics, industrial lighting, handmade textiles, garden ornaments and vintage paintings.

Farrow & Ball
www.farrow-ball.com
Richly pigmented paint in timeless shades and handcrafted wallpaper.

Goose Home and Garden
www.goosehomeandgarden.com
@goosehomeandgarden
+44 (0)7981 268427
Beautiful vintage furniture, decorative antiques and garden accessories.

Gil Fox Hats
www.etsy.com/uk/shop/gilfoxhats
@gilfoxhats
Milliner and maker of vintage-style hats, berets and accessories.

Hannah Watchorn England
www.hannahwatchorn.com
Illustrations, hand-lettering and printed textiles.

Julia Burgan
@juliaburgan
Upholsterer using vintage linens.

Kate Forman
www.kateforman.co.uk
Pretty printed linens, cottons, velvets, wallpapers and home accessories.

The Little Greene Company
www.littlegreene.co.uk
The Colours of England collection is a range of 128 classic and contemporary paint colours.

Lois Kirsten
@lois.kirsten
Vintage and antique trinkets and treasures.

Nutley Antiques
Libra House
High Street
Nutley TN22 3NF
@nutleyantiques
Home to 11 antique and vintage dealers in the heart of the Ashdown Forest, East Sussex.

Piglet in Bed
www.pigletinbed.com
Durable linen bedding and pyjamas that get softer and softer with wear.

Rachel Ashwell
www.shabbychic.com
Inspiration from the creator of Shabby Chic™.

Robert Kime
190–192 Ebury Street
London SW1W 8UP
www.robertkime.com
Wallpapers, fabrics and accessories from the celebrated decorator.

Rosebud & Violet
@rosebudandviolet
Time-worn treasures for your home.

Rosiebud Decorative
@rosiebuddecorative
Decorative antiques, pretty homeware and soft furnishings.

Roundhill Shepherd Huts
www.roundhillshepherdhuts.co.uk
Traditionally made shepherd's huts, many created using antique furnishings, cupboards and floors.

Sea Garden
3 River Street
Portscatho
Cornwall TR2 5HQ
+44 (0)1872 580847
talesfromtheseagarden.blogspot.com
*A carefully curated collection of the
antique and handmade.*

Spencer Swaffer Antiques
30 High Street
Arundel BN18 9AB
+44 (0)1903 882132
spencerswaffer.co.uk
*Antique furniture, mirrors, garden
furniture, lighting and objects.
A favourite port of call for many
top dealers and decorators.*

Stable Antiques
46 West Street
Storrington
Pulborough RH20 4EE
Stableantiques.co.uk
*A large collection of antiques and vintage
sellers homed in a beautiful old house.*

**Sugar & Spice Lifestyle and Home
Furnishings**
sugarandspicefurnishings.co.uk
*Handmade curtains, blinds, eiderdowns
and soft furnishings designed and delivered
throughout the UK and Europe.*

Weathered & Worn
High Street
Hadlow
Kent TN11 0EF
weatheredandworn.me
*Antiques, decorative vintage homewares
and textiles plus a small rustic coffee shop.*

Wild Willow Flowers
wild-willow.co.uk
*Wild Willow creates beautiful flowers for
weddings as well as offering unique styling,
prop hire and hand-crafted wreaths.*

The Woven Agency
wovenstore.com
@wovenstoreonline
*Timeless, beautifully crafted clothing
that stands the test of time.*

BUSINESS CREDITS

Sophie Bateman
@sophie_b_in_sussex
*Pages 2, 18, 28 above right, 36 left,
39 below right, 106–117.*

Amanda Daughtry
@mysimplehome
&
Belle Daughtry
@just_belle
www.belledaughtry.com
*Pages 15 above right, 15 centre left, 15
below left, 19 above left, 19 centre left,
23 centre, 26 centre, 48–57.*

Stephanie Eley
@Pearlyhill_
*Pages 3, 16 above right, 16 centre left,
16 below left, 17, 20 centre left, 24 above,
26 right, 27, 29, 35 right, 37, 41 above
right, 92–105.*

Michelle Essam
Found Country Antiques
@michelle.foundcountryantiques
Pages 12, 13 below left, 44 below, 138–145.

Emma Gurmin
V R Interiors
E: emma@velvetribbon.co.uk
www.velvetribbon.co.uk

@v_r_interiors
*Front endpapers right, pages 1, 13 above
right, 15 below right, 20 above right,
26 left, 28 below right, 36 right, 39 above
right, 46–47, 146–155, back endpapers left.*

Lucy Haywood
The Country Brocante Events
www.thecountrybrocante.co.uk
@thecountrybrocante
and
@Lucyhaywoodathome
*Front endpapers left, pages 4, 5 centre, 6–9,
13 above left, 13 below right, 14, 15 centre
right, 16 above left, 16 below right, 19
above right, 19 centre right, 20 above left,
20 centre right, 20 below, 28 above left,
38, 39 above left.*

Mora Lifestyle
An independent shop in Upper St Giles,
Norwich with a handpicked range of
beautiful clothing, accessories and
decorative items.
95 Upper St Giles
Norwich NR2 1AB
www.moralifestyle.co.uk
@moralifestyle
*Pages 16 centre right, 24 below left, 25, 28
below left, 41 below, 44 above, 45, 66–77.*

Rosehip in the Country
Online shop, open studios and fairs
www.rosehipinthecountry.com
@rosehipinthecountry
and
Kate Nicole
Oyster Bridge & Co
E: oysterbridgeandco@gmail.com
www.oysterbridgeandco.tumblr.com
@oysterbridgeandco
*Pages 5 above, 21–23 left, 23 right,
30, 31 left, 34, 35 left, 36 centre, 42,
78–91.*

**John Taylor and Barbara Cunnell
of Woodpigeon**
Painted furniture and decorative
antiques.
E: thewoodpigeon@btinternet.com
@woodpigeon_1
*Pages 24 below right, 31 centre,
39 below left, 43, 128–137.*

Caroline Zoob Designs
www.carolinezoob.co.uk
@carolinezoobdesign
*Pages 10–11, 19 below left, 31 right,
32–33, 35 centre, 39 above centre,
39 below centre, 40, 58–65.*

PICTURE CREDITS

Front endpapers left The Country Brocante Fair; Front endpapers right The London home of Emma Gurmin; 1 The London home of Emma Gurmin; 2 The home of Sophie Bateman and family in West Sussex; 3 The home and homestead of Stephanie Eley in Oxfordshire; 4 Lucy Haywood's home in the country; 5 above Rosehip in the Country www.rosehipinthecountry.com; 5 centre The Country Brocante Fair; 6–9 The Country Brocante Fair; 10–11 The home of the designer and embroiderer Caroline Zoob in Sussex; 12 Michelle Essam's home In Sussex; 13 above left The Country Brocante Fair; 13 above right The London home of Emma Gurmin; 13 below left Michelle Essam's home In Sussex; 13 below right Lucy Haywood's home in the country; 14 The Country Brocante Fair; 15 above left Susannah and Mark Adorian; 15 above right and 15 centre left A country cottage in Suffolk, the home of Amanda and Belle Daughtry; 15 centre right The Country Brocante Fair; 15 below left A country cottage in Suffolk, the home of Amanda and Belle Daughtry; 15 below right The London home of Emma Gurmin; 16 above left The Country Brocante Fair; 16 above right and 16 centre left The home and homestead of Stephanie Eley in Oxfordshire; 16 centre right The home of Jon and Louise Bunning of Mora Lifestyle, Norwich; 16 below left The home and homestead of Stephanie Eley in Oxfordshire; 16 below right The Country Brocante Fair; 17 The home and homestead of Stephanie Eley in Oxfordshire; 18 The home of Sophie Bateman and family in West Sussex; 19 above left and 19 centre left A country cottage in Suffolk, the home of Amanda and Belle Daughtry; 19 above right and 19 centre right The Country Brocante Fair; 19 below left The home of the designer and embroiderer Caroline Zoob in Sussex; 19 below right Susannah and Mark Adorian; 20 above left, 20 centre right and 20 below The Country Brocante Fair; 20 above right The London home of Emma Gurmin; 20 centre left The home and homestead of Stephanie Eley in Oxfordshire; 21–23 left Rosehip in the Country www.rosehipinthecountry.com; 23 centre A country cottage in Suffolk, the home of Amanda and Belle Daughtry; 23 right Rosehip in the Country www.rosehipinthecountry.com; 24 above The home and homestead of Stephanie Eley in Oxfordshire; 24 below left The home of Jon and Louise Bunning of Mora Lifestyle, Norwich; 24 below right The home in Arundel of John Taylor and Barbara Cunnell of Woodpigeon; 25 The home of Jon and Louise Bunning of Mora Lifestyle, Norwich; 26 left The London home of Emma Gurmin; 26 centre A country cottage in Suffolk, the home of Amanda and Belle Daughtry; 26 right and 27 The home and homestead of Stephanie Eley in Oxfordshire; 28 above left The Country Brocante Fair; 28 above right The home of Sophie Bateman and family in West Sussex; 28 below left The home of Jon and Louise Bunning of Mora Lifestyle, Norwich; 28 below right The London home of Emma Gurmin; 29 The home and homestead of Stephanie Eley in Oxfordshire; 30 and 31 left Rosehip in the Country www.rosehipinthecountry.com; 31 centre The home in Arundel of John Taylor and Barbara Cunnell of Woodpigeon; 31 right The home of the designer and embroiderer Caroline Zoob in Sussex; 32–33 The home of the designer and embroiderer Caroline Zoob in Sussex; 34 and 35 left Rosehip in the Country www.rosehipinthecountry.com; 35 centre The home of the designer and embroiderer Caroline Zoob in Sussex; 35 right The home and homestead of Stephanie Eley in Oxfordshire; 36 left The home of Sophie Bateman and family in West Sussex; 36 centre Rosehip in the Country www.rosehipinthecountry.com; 36 right The London home of Emma Gurmin; 37 The home and homestead of Stephanie Eley in Oxfordshire; 38 Lucy Haywood's home in the country; 39 above left The Country Brocante Fair; 39 above centre The home of the designer and embroiderer Caroline Zoob in Sussex; 39 above right The London home of Emma Gurmin; 39 below left The home in Arundel of John Taylor and Barbara Cunnell of Woodpigeon; 39 below centre The home of the designer and embroiderer Caroline Zoob in Sussex; 39 below right The home of Sophie Bateman and family in West Sussex; 40 The home of the designer and embroiderer Caroline Zoob in Sussex; 41 above left Susannah and Mark Adorian; 41 above right The home and homestead of Stephanie Eley in Oxfordshire; 41 below The home of Jon and Louise Bunning of Mora Lifestyle, Norwich; 42 Rosehip in the Country www.rosehipinthecountry.com; 43 The home in Arundel of John Taylor and Barbara Cunnell of Woodpigeon; 44 above The home of Jon and Louise Bunning of Mora Lifestyle, Norwich; 44 below Michelle Essam's home In Sussex; 45 The home of Jon and Louise Bunning of Mora Lifestyle, Norwich; 46–47 The London home of Emma Gurmin; 48–57 A country cottage in Suffolk, the home of Amanda and Belle Daughtry; 58–65 The home of the designer and embroiderer Caroline Zoob in Sussex; 66–77 The home of Jon and Louise Bunning of Mora Lifestyle, Norwich; 78–91 Rosehip in the Country www.rosehipinthecountry.com; 92–105 The home and homestead of Stephanie Eley in Oxfordshire; 106–117 The home of Sophie Bateman and family in West Sussex; 118–127 Susannah and Mark Adorian; 128–137 The home in Arundel of John Taylor and Barbara Cunnell of Woodpigeon; 138–145 Michelle Essam's home In Sussex; 146–155 The London home of Emma Gurmin; Back endpapers left The London home of Emma Gurmin; Back endpapers right The Country Brocante Fair.

INDEX

Page numbers in *italic* refer to the illustrations

ACKNOWLEDGMENTS

The Country Brocante is a beautiful business that is full of the most wonderful exhibitors and visitors. Without your participation, passion and creativity the business and this book would never have come to fruition.

I would like to thank my wonderful husband who never fails to be full of encouragement and support: nothing is ever too much trouble, from managing unloading at the fair to keeping us all fed and happy.

I had the most wonderful time visiting the homes of the exhibitors and visitors; I am so grateful to you all for opening your homes to us and making us feel so welcome. Each home will hold really special memories for me. I loved hearing about how your homes came about, the love and attention to detail in creating them. It was fabulous to travel and visit new places.

Special thanks go to my wonderful team at The Country Brocante – Clara Sewell-Knight and Clare Lloyd who are my rocks, their never-failing commitment to the business, their humour, support and relentless work ethic ensures everything runs like clockwork and looks amazing.

To Sophie Bateman who has been instrumental in getting this project finished, for helping me write and get my words out of my head and onto paper.

Ben Edwards who took the most exquisite pictures, put up with the ridiculousness of me and had the patience of a saint.

Annabel Haywood, who allowed me to focus on this book whilst she took the reins building our show at Daylesford.

Jess Walton who put me forward for this project and encouraged me to pitch the idea. Annabel Morgan for her patient editing, Toni Kay for the beautiful design and publisher Cindy Richards, for allowing me the time to create this book alongside our busy fair schedule: I am so grateful.

My wonderful creative parents and sister who are a constant source of inspiration to me and always front line for everything Country Brocante.

And last but not least, my gorgeous daughters, Daisy and Florrie – it is all for you my magical little beings.